WHAT'S BODY IMAGE?

By Jennifer Lombardo

Published in 2025 by
KidHaven Publishing, an Imprint of Greenhaven Publishing, LLC
2544 Clinton Street
Buffalo, NY 14224

Designer: Deanna Lepovich
Editor: Jennifer Lombardo

Photo credits: Cover (top) Daisy Daisy/Shutterstock.com; cover (bottom) DisobeyArt/Shutterstock.com; p. 5 New Africa/Shutterstock.com; p. 7 Irina Strelnikova/Shutterstock.com; p. 9 indira's work/Shutterstock.com; p. 11 VGstockstudio/Shutterstock.com; p. 13 Rizar el pixel/Shutterstock.com; p. 15 Nejron Photo/Shutterstock.com; p. 17 Jacob Lund/Shutterstock.com; p. 19 Ground Picture/Shutterstock.com; p. 21 CARACOLLA/Shutterstock.com.

Cataloging-in-Publication Data

Names: Lombardo, Jennifer.
Title: What's body image? / Jennifer Lombardo.
Description: Buffalo, New York : KidHaven Publishing, 2025. | Series: What's the issue? | Includes glossary and index.
Identifiers: ISBN 9781534547940 (pbk.) | ISBN 9781534547957 (library bound) | ISBN 9781534547964 (ebook)
Subjects: LCSH: Body image–Juvenile literature.
Classification: LCC BF724.3.B55 L66 2025 | DDC 155.2–dc23

Printed in the United States of America

CPSIA compliance information: Batch #CSKH25: For further information contact Greenhaven Publishing LLC at 1-844-317-7404.

Please visit our website, www.greenhavenpublishing.com. For a free color catalog of all our high-quality books, call toll free 1-844-317-7404 or fax 1-844-317-7405.

Find us on

CONTENTS

Thoughts and Feelings

The way a person thinks and feels about their body is their body image. These thoughts and feelings are **influenced** by many different things. Who you are as a person, or your personality, is one of them. Another is the messages you get about your body from friends, family members, and the **media**.

Having a positive body image means you feel good about your body most of the time. You like how it looks and feels. Having a negative, or bad, body image means you don't feel good about your body.

Facing the Facts

About 45 percent of children and teens say they aren't happy with how their body looks.

People who are active often have a better body image than people who aren't very active. Having fun moving their body often helps people **appreciate** their body for what it can do.

Physical and Mental

Having a positive body image is important. People who feel good about their body tend to have better physical and mental health. Physical health deals with your body. Usually, a person with good physical health is not sick very often. When they do get sick, they get better quickly.

Mental health deals with your mind. People with good mental health usually are happier and have an easier time dealing with negative emotions, or feelings. Our mental and physical health are connected. When we have problems with one, we are likely to have problems with the other too.

Facing the Facts 🔍

Just like bodies can get sick, minds can have health problems too. In the United States, about 7.7 million children and teens have a mental illness or disorder.

Signs of Poor Mental Health

- low or no **energy**
- trouble remembering important things
- fighting with friends and family
- thinking about hurting yourself or someone else
- inability to stop thinking about sad or scary things
- going from happy to sad or angry very quickly and for what seems like no reason
- eating or sleeping too much or too little
- feeling like nothing matters
- feeling angry at yourself for being who you are

Poor body image is one thing that can cause poor mental health. If you're dealing with one or more of the things on this list, even if you don't feel like you have poor body image, talk to a trusted adult.

Mixed Messages

The messages we get about how our bodies should look and how we should feel about them are often confusing. One day, you might see a post that says to love yourself no matter what you look like. The next day, you might hear someone making fun of how someone looks.

The way our friends, family, and the media talk about bodies can have a big **impact** on how we see ourselves. In many countries, people get the message that the ideal, or best, way to look is to be tall, young, and thin, with shiny hair, smooth skin, and a **symmetrical** face.

Facing the Facts

Even though media might send the message that there's one ideal way to look, everyone has different ideas about what makes a person beautiful, and beauty has nothing to do with someone's worth.

Many people base their ideas of beauty on fashion models, actors, and other famous people. Someone who doesn't fit this type may have a negative body image.

Bodies and Food

Someone with a negative body image might start to have bad feelings about food. When people get the message that it's best to be very thin, they sometimes try to lose weight in dangerous, or unsafe, ways or amounts.

An eating disorder is a mental and physical illness. A person with an eating disorder often has a **distorted** body image. They often fear gaining weight, even when they're thin enough to make them sick. For some, eating disorders are more about control. Someone who feels like they don't have control over many things in their life might try to take control over when and what they eat.

Facing the Facts

People between the ages of 12 and 25 make up 95 percent of people with one or more known eating disorders.

Anorexia is one kind of eating disorder. A person
with anorexia doesn't eat enough food to keep them healthy,
and they are often very afraid of gaining weight.

Bodies and Exercise

Moving the body is important for physical and mental health. However, someone with a negative body image can take it too far. A healthy amount of movement can leave a person feeling tired—but in a good way. People who move in a healthy way also know the importance of rest.

An unhealthy amount of movement leaves a person tired in a way that feels bad. Exercising for too long every day can injure, or hurt, someone because their muscles never get a chance to rest and heal. It's also unsafe to exercise without plenty of water and without food to power the movement.

Facing the Facts

Some people use too much exercise to **punish** themselves for not having their ideal body. This is a sign of poor mental health caused by poor body image.

Someone who exercises too much
can make themselves too tired to do anything else.

13

A Distorted View

The messages we get about our bodies are often sneaky—so sneaky, in fact, that we sometimes don't even notice how they're making our body image worse. When adults make comments about how little they like their bodies, kids often start to have negative thoughts about their own bodies.

Seeing people who fit the beauty ideal in movies and TV can also make people unhappy with how they look. Even if no one tells them they must look the same way, people often make a connection in their minds between beauty and success.

Facing the Facts

In 2021, companies that pushed people to lose weight made around $224.27 billion. Because these companies want to keep making money, they keep sending the message that thin bodies are ideal.

Kids whose parents make comments about how much they're eating are more likely to have a negative body image as they grow.

Don't Compare

Bodies naturally come in a **variety** of shapes, sizes, and colors. Comparing ourselves to other people can lead to poor body image, especially when we can't look just like them. Social media has made this problem worse.

Filters on Instagram, Snapchat, TikTok, and other apps can make people look different than they do in real life. Some people put a filter on their pictures or videos and pretend it's how they always look. For magazines and ads, people often use a computer program called Photoshop to give models, actors, and musicians the "ideal" face and body.

Facing the Facts

The media often sends the message that lighter skin is prettier than darker skin. This can give people of color a negative body image, even in countries where most people have dark skin.

There's no "right" way to look.
Everyone is beautiful in their own way!

Better Body Image

Most of us are harder on ourselves than we are on other people. Most people don't even notice the things we don't like about our bodies. We also don't often notice those things about other people.

Making our body image better can be very hard. A good way to start is by not saying negative things about your body or anyone else's. In time, it will get easier to start saying positive things. Treating your body well by giving yourself the right amount of food, movement, and rest can also help.

Facing the Facts

When COVID-19 spread around the world, many people spent more time than ever on social media. This had a big negative impact on body image, especially for young girls.

If you don't feel good about your body, try talking to friends you trust. They can help you feel better about the way you look. They probably have felt the same way at one time or another.

Making a Change

It can be very hard for people to change their body image. Every day, people get messages about the ways their body is different from the "ideal" body. Don't get angry at yourself if you don't feel better right away. Try to remember that everyone gets those messages. Even people who fit the "ideal" need to work to see themselves positively!

Everyone's body changes over time. Keeping a positive body image through those changes will be hard on some days and easy on others. Finding ways to make yourself feel better and focus on what you like about yourself will help you have more good days than bad.

Facing the Facts 🔍

Body positivity involves feeling positively about how your body looks. Body neutrality involves accepting your body for what it is and what it can do.

WHAT CAN YOU DO?

Talk to a trusted adult if negative body image is harming your mental health.

Treat your body with love and respect.

Limit your time on social media.

Speak kindly about your body, and invite others to do the same about theirs.

Honor the good things about your personality, not just your looks.

Replace negative thoughts about your body with positive ones.

Try to avoid, or stay away from, talking about anyone else's body.

Don't compare yourself to other people.

Changing the way you think about your body can help you change the way you feel about it.

GLOSSARY

appreciate: To be grateful for and see the worth of something.

distorted: Twisted out of a natural, normal, or original shape or condition.

energy: The ability to do work.

filter: A digital effect that changes the way an image looks.

impact: A strong effect.

influence: To have an effect on.

media: Forms or systems of communication, such as TV, books, and ads, designed to reach a large number of people.

punish: To make someone suffer for real or imagined wrongdoing.

symmetrical: Looking the same on both sides of an imaginary center line.

variety: A number or collection of different things.

FOR MORE INFORMATION

WEBSITES

Kids Helpline: Developing a Positive Body Image

kidshelpline.com.au/teens/issues/developing-positive-body-image

Learn more about what it means to have a positive body image.

YouTube: Reverse Selfie

www.youtube.com/watch?v=z2T-Rh838GA

This commercial from a company called Dove shows how people can change the way they look on social media.

BOOKS

Hammond, Mel. *Body Image: How to Love Yourself, Live Life to the Fullest, and Celebrate All Kinds of Bodies*. Middleton, WI: American Girl Publishing, 2022.

Hohn, Tierra. *Body Image: Because All Bodies Are Great Bodies*. Toronto, Ontario: James Lorimer & Company Ltd., 2021.

Wilder, Adelaide. *Body Image*. Vancouver, British Columbia: Engage Books, 2023.

INDEX